BACKHOUSES
OF THE
NORTH

WRITTEN AND ILLUSTRATED BY

MURIEL E. NEWTON-WHITE

PUBLISHED BY
HIGHWAY BOOK SHOP
COBALT, ONTARIO, CANADA.

Frontispiece:

An Ancient and Venerable Back-house which has recently been restored and is being preserved as a historic monument.

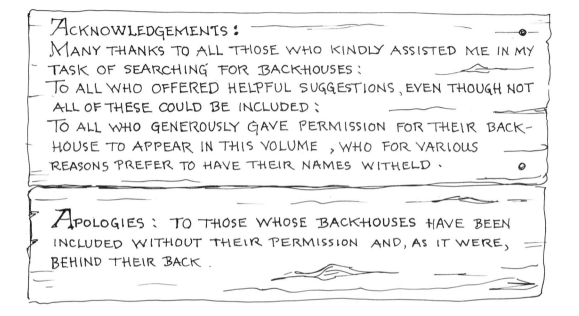

Acknowledgements:
MANY THANKS TO ALL THOSE WHO KINDLY ASSISTED ME IN MY TASK OF SEARCHING FOR BACKHOUSES:
TO ALL WHO OFFERED HELPFUL SUGGESTIONS, EVEN THOUGH NOT ALL OF THESE COULD BE INCLUDED:
TO ALL WHO GENEROUSLY GAVE PERMISSION FOR THEIR BACK-HOUSE TO APPEAR IN THIS VOLUME, WHO FOR VARIOUS REASONS PREFER TO HAVE THEIR NAMES WITHELD.

Apologies: TO THOSE WHOSE BACKHOUSES HAVE BEEN INCLUDED WITHOUT THEIR PERMISSION AND, AS IT WERE, BEHIND THEIR BACK.

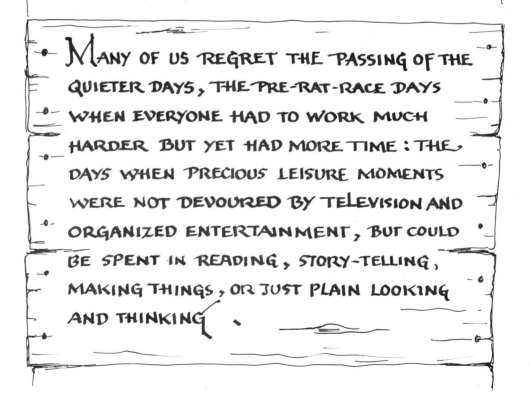

MANY OF US REGRET THE PASSING OF THE
QUIETER DAYS, THE PRE-RAT-RACE DAYS
WHEN EVERYONE HAD TO WORK MUCH
HARDER BUT YET HAD MORE TIME: THE
DAYS WHEN PRECIOUS LEISURE MOMENTS
WERE NOT DEVOURED BY TELEVISION AND
ORGANIZED ENTERTAINMENT, BUT COULD
BE SPENT IN READING, STORY-TELLING,
MAKING THINGS, OR JUST PLAIN LOOKING
AND THINKING.

If we want to find one particular symbol for those good old days, there is nothing better than

THE BACKHOUSE.

It symbolizes the hard work, thrift, quietness, and spirit of adventure that help to make up the charm of rural and small-town life.

Outdoor Conveniences

It was a good life.... Old-time

  backhouse-owners could take advantage of the seclusion of the backhouse to sit and browse through the things they would like to have ordered from last year's catalogue, or to re-read the short story in last month's farm paper..... ~~~ Owners of modern bathrooms, on the other hand, have time for business only; such things as water-rates and bills for bathroom fixtures keep them under constant pressure.

BACKHOUSES ARE SELF-SUPPORTING, EXCEPT ON HALLOWE'EN; AND, BECAUSE THEY CONTRIBUTE GREATLY TO SOIL ENRICHMENT, THEY CAN BE CONSIDERED A DEFINITE ASSET; ALBEIT A FROZEN ONE IN WINTER. BATHROOMS, ALAS, DO NOTHING EXCEPT CONSUME PURE WATER AND TURN IT INTO SEWAGE.

THIS OBLIGING BACKHOUSE NOT ONLY SUPPORTS THE WOODPILE BUT ALSO HOLDS UP THE CLOTHESLINE, ALTHOUGH IT HAS RETIRED FROM ITS OTHER DUTIES.

THE BEAUTY OF BACKHOUSES IS FREQUENTLY ENHANCED BY LOVELY SURROUNDINGS SUCH AS BRIGHT FLOWER-GARDENS; WHILE THEY IN TURN NEVER FAIL TO ENRICH THEIR SURROUNDINGS.... FLOWERS GROW WELL HERE.

The backhouse is a peaceful place. Generally, the path leading to it is a narrow winding one, sheltered either by trees and bushes or by sheds and woodpiles. In a well-sheltered situation one can even leave the door open and sit there enjoying the beauties of Nature.... One can dream there, and meditate; sorrows can be taken there to be wept over in secret; angers and hurts can be recovered from there.

Its doorway frames a delightful view of the Blanche River.

A woodland backhouse, built of logs and set into the side of a hill: It is easily mistaken for a root-cellar or a well. This is not as serious as mistaking a root-cellar or well for a backhouse.

THE BACK FORTY

OF COURSE ONE MUST ADMIT THAT THERE ARE DRAWBACKS TO BACKHOUSES. WASPS LIKE TO NEST IN THEM, AND BEES UNDER THEM - UNDER THE FRONT ENTRANCE, THAT IS. THEY ARE DEARLY LOVED BY MOSQUITOES AND BLACK FLIES.

IF YOU HAVE A LADY VISITOR FROM TOWN SHE IS SURE TO ENCOUNTER A MOUSE OR A SNAKE THERE.

AT NIGHT, BACKHOUSES ARE HAUNTED BY SHADOWS THAT ONE MISTAKES FOR BEARS - OR, WORSE STILL, BY BEARS THAT ONE MISTAKES FOR SHADOWS.

WHO WHO WHOO?

Sometimes someone will inadvertently, or otherwise, lock you in.

Sometimes the backhouse will be visited at night by a hungry porcupine, to whom well worn seats are a great delicacy. The result has to be sand-papered.

Then, there is nothing worse than a skunk who parks himself in the trail outside, just as you are ready to leave; unless it is the skunk you find waiting for you on the doorstep when you want in the worst way to go in.

OCCUPATIONAL HAZARDS

—AND WHAT'S FOR DESSERT?

13

Winter brings many problems. After a heavy snowfall it can take a long time to dig out the backhouse, and delay can have serious consequences. On an extremely cold morning one can freeze to the seat, and that is bad. But the greatest tragedy of all is to be too cold to stop and read the end of a thrilling story before one is obliged to make ends meet.

YES, THERE ARE TIMES WHEN EVEN THE MOST ARDENT BACKHOUSE-LOVER, WHO IS GENERALLY A DOWN-TO-EARTH PERSON WILLING TO FACE REALITIES, WILL ADMIT TO A SECRET LONGING FOR INDOOR CONVENIENCES. ON THE OTHER HAND, HOW DRAB, HOW UNEXCITING, IS A BACKHOUSELESS EXISTENCE! THE INDOOR CONVENIENCE IS MONOTONOUSLY THE SAME, DAY AND NIGHT, SUMMER AND WINTER, AND CAN NEVER DO MORE THAN SERVE A STRICTLY UTILITARIAN PURPOSE; WHILE A VISIT TO THE BACKHOUSE IS FRAUGHT WITH INTEREST, EXCITEMENT, AND ~ DANGER.

Unfortunately there is grave danger that the backhouse may become extinct. It is already rare in many localities. In order to avert this disaster, the Society for Preservation Of Outhouses has been formed. Members are urged to form local Backhouse-watchers' Clubs, to foster interest among young people. This can be a fascinating hobby, and many a young traveller can be kept happy on a long journey by watching for and identifying backhouses.

The Society also urges its members to build or purchase backhouses of their own. If you are considering such an investment, you will have an important decision to make: should the backhouse of your choice have a pit, or a pail? If it has a pit, it will have to be moved once in a while to a new location. If it has a pail, you must be prepared for the task of emptying this. When the path is slippery it is advisable to let someone else do it.

FOR THE BENEFIT OF THOSE WHO WISH TO
MAKE AN IN-DEPTH STUDY OF THE SUBJECT,
THE FOLLOWING PAGES OF NOTES AND SKETCHES
ARE OFFERED AS A GUIDE. IT MIGHT BE AS
WELL, THOUGH, TO WARN THESE ENTHUSIASTS
NOT TO GO IN TOO DEEP. ON THE OTHER HAND
A RUDIMENTARY KNOWLEDGE IS ESSENTIAL TO
ALL, BECAUSE THERE ARE MANY VARIETIES OF
BACKHOUSE IN THE NORTH, AND IN SOME
CASES IT IS DIFFICULT TO DISTINGUISH THEM
FROM OTHER OUTBUILDINGS. AND THERE ARE
OCCASIONS WHEN IT IS NECESSARY TO MAKE
THIS DISTINCTION AT VERY SHORT NOTICE.

IS IT, OR IS IT NOT?

IN THIS INSTANCE,
DEFINITELY NOT.

THE STUDENT OF BACKHOUSES SHOULD BEGIN BY LEARNING CAREFULLY THE MANY OTHER NAMES BY WHICH THIS EDIFICE IS KNOWN :

THE OUTHOUSE :   THE LITTLE HOUSE :
THE WEE HOUSE :   THE OUTDOOR INCONVENIENCE :
THE HOUSE OF PARLIAMENT :   AUNTIE :
THE COMFORT STATION :   THE WHAT-YOU-CALL-IT :
THE BACK FORTY :   THE JOHN :
OUT BACK :   THE TOILET :
THE W. C. (AN ENGLISH EUPHEMISM, SHORT FOR WATER CLOSET)
THE PRIVY :   THE JONES' HOUSE

AND
THERE
ARE
OTHER
NAMES.

In Québec, and in many Ontario settlements, it is usually called Les Bécosses. It is generally believed that this name originated as a result of the Englishman's habit of dropping H's and shortening long vowels, especially when he is in a hurry.

You will also find : (IN TIME, WE HOPE)

LA TOILETTE:

LE CABINET D'AISANCE:

L'APPARTEMENT DE SOULAGEMENT:

Il n'y a pas d'autre sorte de nom. Si l'on en a besoin, on doit se servir d'un nom anglais.

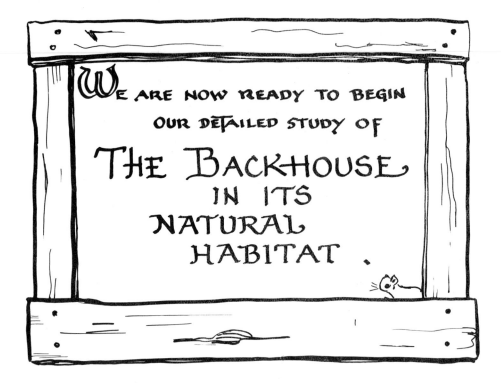

WE ARE NOW READY TO BEGIN
OUR DETAILED STUDY OF
THE BACKHOUSE
IN ITS
NATURAL
HABITAT .

THE CLASSIC BACKHOUSE
IS TALL, SLENDER, AND
WELL-PROPORTIONED.

NOTE THE VARIOUS STYLES
OF VENTILATOR

THE GABLE ROOF
IS ATTRACTIVE -

21

— BUT THE MOST
USUAL
BACKHOUSE
HAS A
LEAN-TO
ROOF ~

CONVENIENT FOR BEING CLIMBED UP

BY VINES AND CREEPERS, AND BY PEOPLE —

—TAKING REFUGE FROM FIERCE DOGS OR ANGRY BULLS. FOR THE LATTER PURPOSE, A LOG BACKHOUSE FACILITATES MATTERS;

BUT THE LOG BACKHOUSE IS BECOMING INCREASINGLY RARE —

~AND THE SHINGLED VARIETY

IS NEARING EXTINCTION .

THE CRESCENT MOON
IS A RARE FIND ~

BUT HAPPILY A
SCENE SUCH AS THIS
IS STILL COMMON IN MOST FARMING
COMMUNITIES.

25

SOME ELDERLY BACKHOUSES LEND MORAL SUPPORT TO
WOODPILES ; OTHERS ARE THEMSELVES IN NEED OF SUPPORT.

THIS UNIQUE SPECIMEN, BOASTING A COTTAGE-
STYLE ROOF, A PICNIC-TABLE (PRESUMABLY),
AND A FEATURE DESCRIBED BY MY YOUNG
COUSIN JIM AS A SMOKE-STACK, IS PROTECTED
BY A LARGE DOG; ∼

~WHILE THE PRIVACY OF THIS ONE IS GUARDED BY A PICKET-FENCE.

Backhouses are expected to take a back seat, so to speak, and for this reason they generally have protective colouring. For this, there is nothing better than the soft grey of weathered wood. However, those who feel that longevity is more desirable for their backhouse than self-effacement, paint it. The most usual colour-scheme is white with green trim; the colour that used to be known as T. & N. O. Ry. Red is quite common; and a few daring backhouses stand out in shocking pink or baby blue.

SOME ARE DISCREETLY HIDDEN
BY THE CORN - PATCH , OR BY
SHRUBS AND TREES.

THE
CHURCH
BACKHOUSE
HIDES
APOLOGETICALLY
IN A
CORNER.

MANY BACKHOUSES LIKE TO CUDDLE CLOSE TO
OTHER OUTBUILDINGS FOR SHELTER.

SOMETIMES IT IS HARD TO TELL WHICH IS WHICH.

In the back lanes of small towns
they are quite neighbourly.

On viewing the backhouse of an old mine, one is struck by its resemblance to the head-frame. Perhaps, in recognition of this, mine backhouses should have a special appellation applied to them.

A MAGNIFICENT SPECIMEN. NOTE THE UNIQUE
FEATURES: THREE AUGER-HOLES IN PLACE OF THE
USUAL SQUARE OR DIAMOND; ALSO, A CEMENT
DOORSTEP. YOU WILL SEE THIS ON YOUR LEFT AS
YOU ENTER THE DRIVEWAY OF THE HIGHWAY
BOOK SHOP. BUT - ITS STANDING DAYS ARE NUMBERED, AS
INSIDE FACILITIES MAKE IT SUPERFLUOUS.

Sadly, many of the finest specimens have been neglected and have fallen into disrepair. In some cases, however, the backhouse has been removed entirely and it is the unwary visitor who has fallen in.

A sad sight.
Before it brings tears to your eyes, look quickly at the next page ~

~ WHICH DEPICTS THE BACKHOUSE FLOURISHING AS ONE OF THE CHIEF JOYS OF THE CAMP .

HERE, IT IS EVEN CELEBRATED IN SONG :
"THE JOHN BRIGADE, THE JOHN BRIGADE,
WE BELONG TO THE JOHN BRIGADE ;
WE TAKE A TIN OF MISTOVAN,
POUR HALF OF A CUP IN A WATER PAN ~ "

FURTHER CONSOLATION MAY BE FOUND IN CONTEMPLATING THIS HANDSOME STRUCTURE, SO RECENTLY COMPLETED THAT THE LADDER FROM WHICH THE ROOF WAS PAPERED HAS NOT YET BEEN REMOVED.

As long as such buildings are being constructed with the exquisite craftsmanship displayed in this example, There is

Hope that the Backhouse may yet survive.

And may the quietness, the pleasure in simple things, the fun and laughter, of the Old Backhouse Days, survive also.

In most books this page would be called the
End-Paper, and would be left blank; but, since in a book
of this nature such a term could lead to misunderstandings
and possible misuse, it is being used for our final
illustration: a colourful backhouse (deep crimson with
apple-green trim), built in the summer of '72 by the
President of the Society.

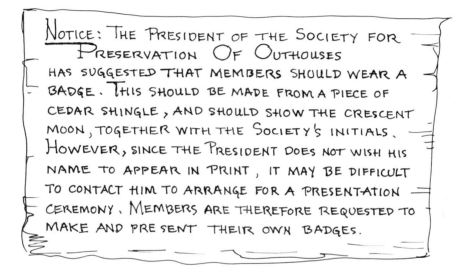

NOTICE: THE PRESIDENT OF THE SOCIETY FOR PRESERVATION OF OUTHOUSES HAS SUGGESTED THAT MEMBERS SHOULD WEAR A BADGE. THIS SHOULD BE MADE FROM A PIECE OF CEDAR SHINGLE, AND SHOULD SHOW THE CRESCENT MOON, TOGETHER WITH THE SOCIETY'S INITIALS. HOWEVER, SINCE THE PRESIDENT DOES NOT WISH HIS NAME TO APPEAR IN PRINT, IT MAY BE DIFFICULT TO CONTACT HIM TO ARRANGE FOR A PRESENTATION CEREMONY. MEMBERS ARE THEREFORE REQUESTED TO MAKE AND PRESENT THEIR OWN BADGES.